Fel

CORAL REEF

WEBS OF LIFE

CORAL REEF

Paul Fleisher

BENCHMARK BOOKS

MARSHALL CAVENDISH
NEW YORK

The author would like to acknowledge Paul Sieswerda of the New York Aquarium for his careful reading. The author also thanks his editor, Kate Nunn. And finally, he would like to thank his wife, Debra, for her support in all things, including the work on this book.

Benchmark Books
Marshall Cavendish Corporation
99 White Plains Road
Tarrytown, New York 10591-9001

Illustration by Jean Cassels

Library of Congress Cataloging-in-Publication Data
Fleisher, Paul.
Coral reef / by Paul Fleisher.
    p.   cm. — (Webs of life)
Includes bibliographical references (p. 39) and index.
Summary: Describes how coral reefs are formed, and some of the many plants and animals that live there.
ISBN 0-7614-0432-5 (lib. bdg.)
1. Coral reef ecology—Juvenile literature. [1. Coral reef ecology. 2. Ecology. 3. Coral reefs and islands.]
I. Title. II. Series: Fleisher, Paul. Webs of life.
QH541.5.C7F54   1998   577.7'89—dc21   97-1932   CIP   AC

Photo research by Ellen Barrett Dudley

Cover photo: The National Audubon Society Collection / Photo Researchers, Inc./ Gregory Ochocki

The photographs in this book are used by permission and through the courtesy of: *The Image Bank*: Armando Jenik, 2; Jeff Hunter, 6-7, 10; Lisy-Schwart, 29 (top). *The National Audubon Society Collection/Photo Researchers, Inc.*: Carl Purcell, 8; Mary Beth Angelo, 9; Michael McCoy, 12; Andrew J. Martinez, 13 (top); Nancy Sefton, 13 (bottom), 18-19, 22; Charles V. Angelo, 21 (top), 24, 25, 31, 35; Mike Neumann, 32. *Peter Arnold, Inc.*: Norbert Wu, 14, 28, 30; Aldo Brando, 15, 34; Kelvin Aitken, 33 (left). *Animals Animals*: W. Gregory Brown, 16-17, 23, 26, 33 (right); Herb Segars, 20; Frank Burek, 21 (bottom); Howard Hall, 29 (bottom).

Printed in the United States of America

6 5 4 3 2 1

For my teachers

A coral reef looks like a brightly colored underwater garden. But most of the beautiful creatures that live here are animals not plants.

Corals are saltwater animals. They live in large groups called colonies. Each coral, or polyp, builds a stony cup in which to live. It makes its limestone shelter from chemicals in the sea. When the polyp dies, it leaves a little bit of rock where it once lived.

Over many years, these little corals build huge, stony reefs. The Great Barrier Reef in Australia can be seen from far out in space. It is the largest structure on earth built by living things—much larger than anything humans have ever made.

GREAT BARRIER REEF

Have you ever seen a jellyfish? A coral is very much like a jellyfish turned upside down. Like jelly-fish, coral catch and eat small animals. They catch some of their food by stinging it with soft fingerlike tentacles. But corals get most of their food in another way.

CORAL REEF
IN THE
CARIBBEAN

Tiny single-celled algae called zooxanthellae (pronounced ZO uh zan THELL ee) live inside each coral animal. Algae are very simple plantlike creatures. The zooxanthellae use sunlight to make food. They make enough food to share with the coral. Coral can't live without them.

Like other plants, zooxanthellae need sunlight. So coral can grow only where the ocean is shallow and warm all year round.

Clear tropical waters are like a desert. The water is crystal blue because very few plants and animals live in it. It has few of the nutrients that plants and animals need to grow. A coral reef is like an oasis of life in the middle of the desert. Reefs are home to more different kinds of creatures than any other place on earth except the rain forest!

Let's visit a reef near an island in the Caribbean Sea. The water is warm, and the sun is shining. We put on our masks and snorkels and swim just above the reef. Be careful to look but not touch. It's very easy to break or damage the delicate coral.

Each kind of coral grows in a different shape. Brain coral forms big boulders. Its twisting lines of polyps make it look like a giant brain.

Staghorn coral grows in the shape of deer antlers. Other corals form pillars or broad, flat plates.

STAGHORN CORAL

BRAIN CORAL (LEFT) AND PLATE FIRE CORAL

PILLAR CORAL

Look closely. Every spot of living space on the reef is taken by some plant or animal. The rocks of the reef are coated with algae. Brightly colored sponges— a very simple kind of animal—grow on the rocks, too. Snails, sea urchins, sea stars, and many kinds of fish graze on the algae and sponges.

VASE SPONGE

FLAMINGO TONGUE SNAIL
FEEDING ON CORAL

Tangs are one of the most common algae eaters. Tangs are also called surgeonfish. The sharp spine on each side of their tails can cut like a surgeon's knife. The spines protect the surgeonfish from other fish that try to eat them.

BLUE TANG

A damselfish claims a patch of algae on the reef as its own. Like a careful farmer, it chases away other fish that enter its territory.

DAMSELFISH DEFENDING ALGAE

The reef protects the lagoon behind it from ocean waves and damaging storms. Sea grasses grow on the shallow sandy bottom. Fish and other animals leave their homes in the reef to feed in the grasses. They graze on algae or hunt for small animals among the waving blades of grass.

A conch crawls across the sandy bottom, scavenging for bits of food. Its heavy shell protects it from hungry fish.

QUEEN CONCH

A goatfish searches for small creatures in the sand.

A sea cucumber—a relative of the sea star—crawls along, gathering sand into its mouth with sticky tentacles. Then it digests bits of food mixed with the sand.

YELLOW GOATFISH

SEA CUCUMBER

SPINY LOBSTER

The reef has many holes where animals can live. A spiny lobster lives in this hole. Lobsters are scavengers. They eat animals that have died and fallen to the bottom of the reef.

An octopus lives in another hole. Its favorite food is lobster. The octopus can change color to match its surroundings. This is called camouflage. Camouflage protects the octopus from its enemies.

OCTOPUS

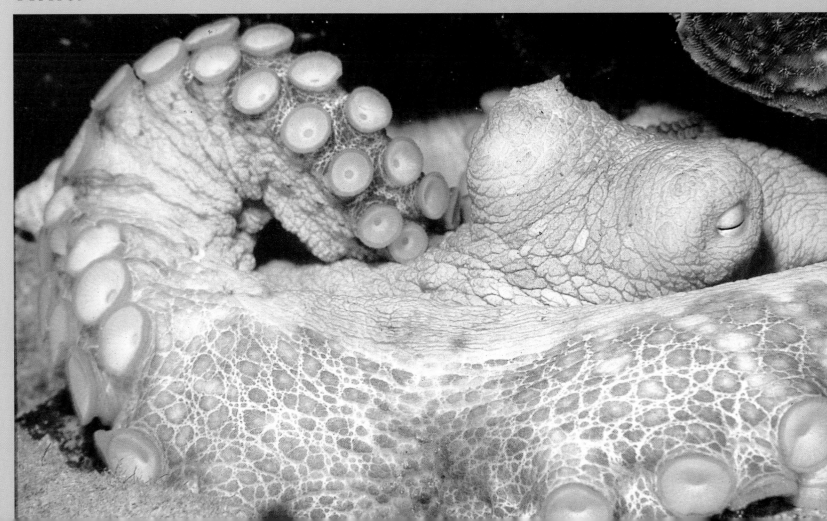

BUTTERFLY FISH

Other reef animals use camouflage, too. Butterfly fish have a false eye spot. When larger fish see the big spot, they think the butterfly fish is bigger than it really is. The spot also confuses predators, or hunters. They don't know which end of the butterfly fish to chase.

GRUNTS

The stripes on these grunts make them hard for a hunting fish to see. They blend with the streaks of sunlight and shadow in the water.

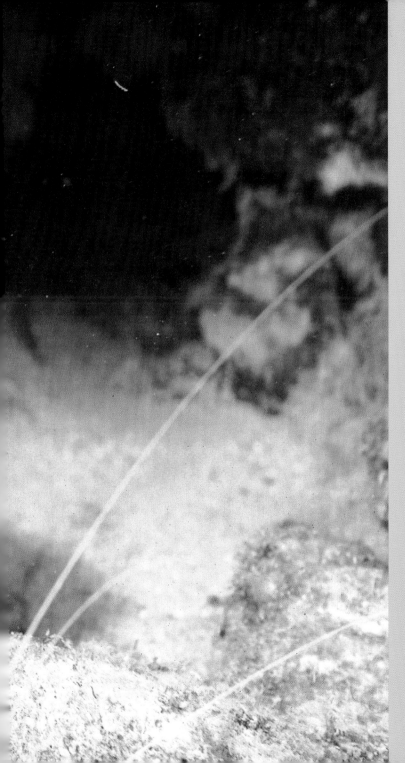

Many reef animals are predators. The moray eel hides in a hole in the reef. It swims out to catch prey with its sharp teeth.

MORAY EEL

BARRACUDAS

REEF SHARK

Barracudas are cruising above the reef looking for a meal.

A gray reef shark is hunting for smaller fish to eat.

Beneath a coral ledge, a large grouper looks for its dinner. Groupers, moray eels, and many other predators do much of their hunting at nightfall.

CONEY RED PHASE GROUPER

ORANGE CLUMP CORAL FEEDING AT NIGHT

The reef looks very different at night. When we shine our underwater light on the reef, even the coral looks different. In the daytime, coral looks like lifeless rock.

But at night, each coral animal puts out its tentacles to capture small swimming animals called plankton.

Animals that were active

during the day find places to hide and rest. Other reef animals come out to hunt when it gets dark.

This squirrelfish spent the day hidden under a shelf of coral. Now it has come out to feed on the plankton. Its big eyes help it spot prey in the dark.

SQUIRRELFISH

Creatures of the reef protect themselves from predators in many different ways. When a porcupine fish is attacked by a bigger fish, it gulps lots of water and puffs up into a spiny ball. Who wants to swallow something this big and prickly?

PORCUPINE FISH, PUFFED UP FOR DEFENSE

FEATHER DUSTER WORMS

NUDIBRANCH

We have to look closely to see these small, colorful feather duster worms. Each worm builds a hard tube to live in. It spreads its feathery tentacles to capture tiny bits of food. When a fish swims near, the worm quickly pulls back into its tube.

Bright colors can be a warning to other creatures. A nudibranch (NOO duh brahnk) is a snail without a shell. The feathery tufts on its body are gills. Many nudibranchs are brightly colored. These nudibranchs may be poisonous to eat.

33

Sometimes reef creatures live and work together. The sea anemone captures prey with stinging tentacles. But cleaner shrimp live safely among the tentacles. The stings don't bother them.

At this cleaning station, a small fish removes tiny, bothersome creatures from the skin of a grouper. The grouper opens its mouth, and the cleaner fish swims right in. The grouper won't eat the cleaner fish. The cleaner fish gets a meal, and the bigger fish stays healthy.

The coral reef gives food and shelter to many animals. Coral reefs are a very important part of the web of life on our earth. A reef is a wonderful place to visit, too.

TIGER GROUPER WITH CLEANER FISH

CLEANER SHRIMP IN ANEMONE

Can you name the animals and corals in this reef?

Turn the page to check your answers.

Animals and Corals Found in This Reef

1. brain coral
2. staghorn coral
3. elkhorn coral
4. plate fire coral
5. pillar coral
6. boulder coral
7. tube sponge

8. finger sponge
9. sea star
10. blue tang
11. damselfish
12. conch
13. goat fish
14. sea cucumber

15. spiny lobster
16. octopus
17. butterfly fish
18. grunt
19. moray eel
20. barracuda
21. reef shark

22. grouper
23. porcupine fish
24. squirrel fish
25. pork fish
26. parrot fish
27. feather duster
28. anemone

FIND OUT MORE

Cousteau Society Staff. *Corals: The Sea's Great Builders*. New York: Simon & Schuster, 1992.

De Larramendi Ruis, Alberto. *Coral Reefs*. Chicago: Childrens Press, 1993.

Gutnik, Martin J. and Natalie Browne-Gutnik. *Great Barrier Reef*. Chatham, NJ: Raintree Steck-Vaughn, 1994.

Pringle, Lawrence. *Coral Reefs*. New York: Simon & Schuster, 1995.

Wood, Jenny. *Coral Reefs*. Milwaukee, WI: Gareth Stevens, 1991.

INDEX

ABOUT THE AUTHOR

In addition to writing children's books, Paul Fleisher teaches gifted middle school students in Richmond, Virginia. He spends many hours outdoors, gardening or fishing on the Chesapeake Bay. One of Fleisher's favorite vacation activities is snorkeling or scuba diving around the coral reefs of the Bahamas and other tropical islands.

Fleisher is active in organizations that work for peace and social justice, including the Richmond Peace Education Center and the Virginia Forum.